The Devotional Life
of the Sunday School Teacher

The Devotional Life

OF THE

Sunday School Teacher

BY

Dr. J.R. Miller

Solid Ground Christian Books
Vestavia Hills, Alabama

SOLID GROUND CHRISTIAN BOOKS
PO Box 660132 ~ Vestavia Hills, AL 35266
e-mail to: solid-ground-books@juno.com
web site: http://solid-ground-books.com
1-877-666-9469 (toll free within N America)
205-978-9469 (all other locations)

The Devotional Life of the Sunday School Teacher
Dr. James Russell Miller (1840-1912)

First published in 1913 by the Presbyterian Board of Publication

Published by Solid Ground Christian Books
© copyright 2002 by Solid Ground Christian Books
All rights reserved

ISBN: 0-9710169-8-4

CONTENTS

Author's Foreword

The real power in Sunday School teaching
is not methods, important as it is to have
the best of these, nor in equipment, valuable
as this is, but in the teacher's own spiritual
life. "Not by might, nor by power, but by my
Spirit," is the divine revealing of the secret
of power in all Christian work.

It is the aim of these simple chapters
to put emphasis upon some of the vital
elements in the Sunday School teacher's
life and work.

J.R. Miller

Biographical Introduction

It is a distinct privilege for Solid Ground Books to be able to bring back before the people of God a choice servant of Christ who has been too long forgotten. J.R. Miller wrote over 60 books, many of which were translated into numerous languages, and which sold multiplied millions of copies. Sir William Robertson Nicoll said of him, "Dr. Miller may be justly called the most popular religious writer of his time...There never, we should suppose, was a man who worked harder." In the following pages we will set forth a brief history of his life, drawing primarily from *The Life of Dr. J.R. Miller* written by his dear friend John T. Faris, and published the year he died (1912).

James Russell Miller was born on March 20, 1840 in the family home near Frankfort Springs, Pennsylvania. He was the first born son of James Alexander Miller and Eleanor Creswell Miller. He was blessed to enter a home that was a house of prayer. From the moment it was founded the family altar was established, and it was never allowed to be broken down. As the children came into the home they soon learned that whatever else might be omitted from the household routine, family worship was never forgotten, and never slighted. Business pressure, the presence of guests, or other trying circumstances were never offered as an excuse for the omission of morning and evening Bible reading and prayer.

In this godly home the Sabbath was sacredly set apart. Seldom, if ever, was the family pew empty, though the church was several miles distant, and the roads were frequently well-nigh impassable. There were no evening services in the churches in those days, but the home became a little sanctuary. The devout father was the minister in his home. Matthew Henry's "Commentary" was taken from the shelf, and his exposition of the text of the evening was read aloud. Then came the reciting of the Westminster Shorter Catechism; as the children grew old enough they were required to learn this as rapidly as possible. Eventually all 107 questions and answers were laid in the hearts of each child, and the father would then begin by proposing the first question to James, who would then answer it, and in turn ask the next child the second question. This would continue until all the questions and answers had been given. Thus the solid doctrinal foundation was laid that lasted the rest of his life.

James was an eager student in school and made great progress. On one occasion he requested of his teacher that algebra be added to the curriculum. The teacher frankly confessed that he knew nothing of the subject, and proposed that both should study it together. Years later that teacher, then an old man, recounted the success of that winter. With the unassuming spirit for which he was always noted, the pupil aided the teacher in understanding the new branch of learning.

Very early in life James began to manifest a deep interest in vital personal religion, and this was intensified during his first winter at Beaver Academy, which he entered in 1857. His fellow students spoke of him as a young man of prayer. He was a regular and devout worshiper in the church, where his voice joined heartily in leading its services of praise. He despised ostentation in religion, yet religion was to him a matter of daily life, and it shone out in every word and deed.

During his academy course he taught one term of school at Industry, Pennsylvania, and another at Calcutta, Ohio, so he did not enter Westminster College at New Wilmington, PA, until 1861. He was so far advanced, however, that he was graduated in June, 1862. In the autumn of that year he entered the theological seminary of the United Presbyterian Church at Allegheny, PA.

Mr. Miller was in college when Fort Sumter fell and the country was plunged into the throes of civil war. He enlisted as a member of a company recruited in and about Calcutta, Ohio. The Lord opened a door of service for him, however, in the newly formed Christian Commission, whose work was outlined as follows:

> The relief and care of the wounded, during and immediately after battle, and meeting the needs of men in such places as parole and convalescent camp, and other emergencies. Also, the supply of religious service in aid of chaplains, or in their place, for hospitals and regiments without chaplains, the supply of reading matter to men in hospitals and throughout the army, the distribution of bodily comforts, and the promotion of communication with home.

This work was carried on by voluntary and paid delegates, under the direction of field agents. Each agent had charge of one army corps, and directed the activities of from five to ten or more delegates. It was in March, 1863 when Mr. Miller - then a middler at Allegheny Seminary - began his service as delegate. He promised to serve for six weeks, but his work was so well done that at the expiration of this period he was urged to remain for the summer campaign. A good situation was waiting for him at home, but he determined to give this up and stay where he felt he was needed more. He was, therefore, assigned to the Army of the Potomac. As Assistant Field Agent, it fell to him, together with two others, to direct the extensive operations of the Commission at Gettysburg after the notable battle fought in July of that same year. Of this service he wrote:

> Every station occupied by the Commission on this field of blood is worthy of a special record. Suffice it to say that at every point of this field, as at others of like character, the effort to relieve the temporal needs was blended with Christian counsel and consolation, and as ever before, so here, the Holy Spirit attended such ministry with the divine blessing.

What was to last for six weeks eventually lasted for two and one half years of service. These years of ministering to the wounded and dying drew forth remarkable gifts in this young man, and fitted him for the world wide ministry of comfort to which he was destined.

Mr. Miller resumed his interrupted studies at Allegheny Theological Seminary in the fall of 1865. His experiences during the war had so broadened his mind and enlarged his heart that he was able to make the most of his opportunities. Fellow students who had valued Mr. Miller because of his unusual attainments marveled at the way in which his character had been enriched by the service of the Christian Commission. They rejoiced in the opportunity for daily fellowship with one who was living so near to heaven that every word and act seemed to lift them close to God. His brotherliness of spirit, his earnestness of purpose, his humility and gentleness, and his never-flagging zeal won the admiration and love of all who knew him.

He completed his course in the spring of 1867, and during the summer he accepted the call from First United Presbyterian Church of New Wilmington, PA, the seat of the college from which he had graduated five years earlier. His ordination and installation took place September 11, 1867, and he at once devoted himself heartily to the work of pulpit and pastorate. Being a college center, the field gave inspiration for the most careful sermon preparation, and men who sat under his preaching in their student days - ministers, doctors, lawyers, and others - told of the uplift which it brought to them. A number of men testified in later years that they were led by his strong personality and the spirit of his work to the determination to devote their lives to the gospel ministry.

It was evident to all who watched his work that he was winning a strong hold upon the hearts of the children, because they always had a warm place in his heart's love. This laid the foundation for his great burden to produce the very best material possible for the Sunday Schools in the years that followed. It also prepared the way for the three gifts the Lord gave to him after marrying Miss Louise E. King on June 22, 1870. From the day of their marriage Mrs. Miller was his inspiration and his helper in all his work. He was never weary of telling of his great debt to her. In his letters to young married people, he frequently told them of what she was to him, and said that he could wish them no greater happiness than a home such as she was making him. The secret of Mrs. Miller's helpfulness was not only her beautiful character, but her recognition of the fact that her husband belonged to those who listened to his preaching, who received him in their home, who read the publications he edited, or who were inspired by his books. That he might be free to serve them she saw to it that he was relieved of all home cares which she could take upon herself. In these efforts she was most successful.

From 1867 until 1912, the year of his death, Mr. Miller was a faithful pastor in several churches. Wherever he went the churches experienced unprecedented growth, especially in conversions. We are told that for his forty years of pastoral labor there was an average of nearly 140 members added every year. These churches grew because of the remarkable, almost superhuman, labors of their pastor. Miller combined the rare gift of being a gifted preacher and a diligent pastor.

As a preacher he was known as one who was faithful to the Scriptures and to the souls of those under his care. He labored to bring the word of God to the consciences of his people, and especially sought to bring comfort and encouragement to the weary. We could not do better than to reproduce a letter that the aged servant of God wrote to a young minister in response to his question about how to make his ministry a success. The letter concluded with these words:

Cultivate love for Christ and then live for your work. It goes without saying that the supreme motive in every minister's life should be the love of Christ. 'The love of Christ constraineth me,' was the keynote of St. Paul's marvelous ministry. But this is not all. If a man is swayed by the love of Christ he must also have in his heart love for his fellow men. If I were to give you what I believe is one of the secrets of my own life, it is, that I have always loved people. I have had an intense desire all of my life to help people in every way; not merely to help them into the church, but to help them in their personal experiences, in their struggles and temptations, their quest for the best things in character. I have loved other people with an absorbing devotion. I have always felt that I should go anywhere, do any personal service, and help any individual, even the lowliest and the highest. The Master taught me this in the washing of the disciples' feet, which showed His heart in being willing to do anything to serve His friends. If you want to have success as a winner of men, as a helper of people, as a pastor of little children, as the friend of the tempted and imperiled, you must love them and have a sincere desire to do them good.

It seems to me that your secret of success just now will be, not in developing the professional ideals, not in following any rules which you have learned in the seminary, but in caring for people with such intensity that you will be ready to make any self-sacrifice to do them good.

This letter was especially valuable because its writer had lived out every statement in it. He loved his people. He forgot himself. He delighted to quote the words of Alexander Maclaren, "To efface self is one of a preacher's first duties." His people loved him because he thought nothing of himself and everything of them.

In addition to his work as a pastor, in 1880 he added the work of assistant to the Editorial Secretary of the Presbyterian Board of Publication. Although small in its beginnings, this was to become the second great calling of his life. It opened the door for his wonderful skills as a writer and caused his name to become a household word in millions of homes in America and abroad. Eventually he became the Editorial Superintendent of the PBP where he faithfully served until the year of his death in 1912. It was here that he poured his life-blood in seeking to bring the Sunday School material to its very highest level possible. The PBP, under his leadership, became the most renowned denominational publishing house in the world. His oversight of this work is all the more remarkable when it is realized that it was carried on while he was also serving as a pastor of a growing church. It was often said that he did the work of three ordinary men. One man was inclined to make the number ten rather than three. His secret was that he never wasted a moment of time, but used each minute for Christ.

One of the gifts that he used to great effect was that of writing personal letters and notes. Dozens of notes and letters went out from his desk every day. Some went across the world, and others across the street. On one occasion, during the evangelistic meetings of R.A. Torrey and Charles Alexander a man stated that the Lord used a note from Dr. Miller to lead him to Christ. On hearing this Mr. Alexander said, "Yes, what a wonderful help Dr. Miller's letters have been to many a weary and troubled soul! I wonder how many persons in this gathering have received letters from Dr. Miller?" One might have expected to see a scattering show of hands here and there throughout the large congregation, but hundreds of hands were raised in silent but eloquent tribute to a man who, although extremely busy, found time to share the burdens and joys of others.

His passion for writing letters continued to the last. One day in May, 1912, while unable to leave his chair because of weakness, he dictated letters to a minister who was celebrating the fiftieth anniversary of his pastorate, to a young man who was that day moving into a new home, to a sick friend, and to a man who had just been highly honored. His last letter - written just a few weeks before his death - was a message of appreciation to an associate. He was so feeble that he fell asleep several times before the letter was completed, but he would not give up until the task was finished.

The secret of his life was summarized in five words that he loved to repeat again and again, "Jesus and I are friends." This was the deepest passion of his life, to know and love Jesus Christ. All he did and all he wrote came from his vital relationship with his Friend. He once wrote in one of his books, "No name of Christ means more to us in the interpretation of His life and love than Friend. We are not only to tell those we teach of the beauty of the friendship of Christ, we must interpret that friendship in ourselves. What Christ was to those to whom He became a personal friend we must be to those we make our friends. He did not seem to do many things for them. He did not greatly change their condition. He did not make life easier for them. It was in a different way that His friendship helped them. He gave them sympathy. They knew He cared for them, and then the hard things meant less to them...The greatest moment in anyone's life is when he first realizes that Christ is his Friend." Thankfully, he was a model of the things he urged others to do. He learned numerous lessons from his Friend. Tens of thousands were made richer because of his desire to pass on what his Friend had taught him.

During his lifetime he wrote 60 books and pamphlets. One of the most amazing things about these volumes is the way they spoke to both the learned and the unlearned, the rich and the poor alike. There seemed to be no hindrance that kept his books from entering into the hearts of children, young people, middle aged and those in old age.

Letters came to him daily for years telling of the good that his books had done. Some are quite remarkable. Consider just a few. One came from a stranger in London, England, who wrote:

> A friend, an architect in Bombay, India, informs me that at Christmas he purchased three hundred copies of your '*Come Ye Apart*' and distributed them among his friends and native clients. One of them went to a Mohammedan prince, for whom he had recently constructed a palace, and in whose house he had great freedom. He afterwards said that the volume was being read with much interest both by the prince and his wife.

Another letter came from the Prime Minister of Great Britain, who wrote,

> Pray accept my thanks for your work on '*The Building of Character*.' It seems to me a work of great value on a subject requiring a skillful hand.   Your very faithful servant, W.E. Gladstone

As moving as it must have been to receive such letters, it meant much more to him to receive the following letter from an anxious mother:

> I have thrown '*The Every Day of Life*' in the way of my son, who is rather careless about reading such books, and I am glad to tell you I often find him reading it. And only this morning at breakfast, when we were talking about the book he remarked, 'I tell you, Dr. Miller is a great man. He knows how to say things that go to the heart.'

A man from Philadelphia visited the palace of the Czar in Russia and he wrote that he saw several of Dr. Miller's books on the reading table of the Czarina. She asked him to say to the author that she had read his books and enjoyed them very much.

The book that you hold in your hand, *The Devotional Life of the Sunday School Teacher*, was not published until after the death of Dr. Miller. In an Explanatory Note in the first edition of the book, we are told,

> The completed manuscript of '*The Devotional Life of the Sunday School Teacher*' was found among the papers of the author after God called him from earth.

This is a book that will be turned to again and again by everyone who cares for the souls of those entrusted to them. It is the mature thought of a man who spent his life seeking to make the Sunday School a vital part in the life and growth of the church. It is not a book of methods, or gimmicks. It will not appeal to those who are more concerned about entertaining children and young people than transforming their lives to be like Christ. It is hoped that an army of men and women will rise up to take the high calling of a Sunday School teacher seriously!

Dr. Miller went to be with his Friend on July 2, 1912. He was 72 years old when he died, and he left behind a legacy that is matched by very few. In closing this brief biographical sketch we will allow some who knew him best to speak of what he meant to them.

Rev. Frank De Witt Talmage wrote,

> I doubt if there is a living minister in all the world who has done a greater work, or who is more internationally known, than Dr. Miller, of this city...In the ecclesiastical life he is the marvel of the age. He has done the work of ten men. While others were attending banquets or sitting by their firesides, his tireless feet have been tramping the streets of the city calling upon the sick and like Paul carrying the gospel into many homes...Of all the great ministers of the past not one has wielded greater influence for good. The whole city should be thankful for the noble life of this wonderful man.

He had already passed beyond the reach of such words as these that came from Dr. F.B. Meyer,

> I hear that my beloved friend is very near his Home-Going. If he is able to hear any human friend whom he has loved, please mention my name to him; tell him that I have loved him and that his love has been sweet. Ask him to look out for me when I come.

Dr. W. Brenton Greene, Professor at Princeton Seminary, after twenty-five years of intimate association with him, said reverently,

> If I dared let any man embody my idea of our Lord, I should find myself unconsciously turning to Dr. Miller for such an embodiment. We can try to follow him only afar off, but it is one of God's best gifts to us that we have been given such an example of Christlikeness.

It is hoped that this brief biographical sketch will prepare you to read the book that you now hold in your hands. It is not a book for cowards. The Sunday School does not need cowards, especially in this evil day in which we live. May the Lord prepare your heart to read the words from this wise servant of a former day, and may they be used to challenge you to greater heights than ever before in your high calling.

The Publisher
April 2002

THE DEVOTIONAL LIFE

OF THE

SUNDAY SCHOOL TEACHER

CHAPTER I

ONE of the most significant words in the teaching of Jesus is that in which he gives his command concerning the care of the children. He asked Peter a question, "lovest thou me?" and when he got a satisfactory answer, he said to him, "Feed my lambs."

He had in mind the figure of a shepherd. David had sung, "The Lord is my shepherd." Jesus himself had used the figure to describe his own tender watchfulness over his people. They are his sheep. The children are the lambs. The word used here means, "little lambs." This suggests that the very youngest children are included. They were infants that were once brought to Jesus, whom the disciples would have kept away, but whom he welcomed so warmly, saying "Suffer the little children, and forbid them not, to come unto me." No mother of

[3]

an infant child should ever feel that the Son of God is too great to care for her baby, to receive it into his arms and to bless it.

An interesting story is told of Francis Xavier, the great Jesuit missionary. Once when throngs were coming to him and he was almost utterly exhausted, he said to his servant: "I must sleep, or I shall die. No matter who comes, do not wake me." Then he crept into his tent and his faithful attendant stood guard. Presently the young man saw his master's pale face at the tent door. Beckoning to him, Xavier said, as if frightened: "I made a mistake! I made a mistake! If a little child comes, waken me." It is thus with our Master. When a little child needs him he is always ready to answer the call.

No flock of lambs in any wilderness is beset by so many perils as are the children in this world. It is the duty of the Church to protect them. The mother is the child's first natural keeper. Every home should be a sanctuary, where the little ones born into it shall be safe. We are careful about health and bodily safety. We make our homes secure shelters from the elements. We look after drainage, ventilation and warmth. We are careful about food, water and clothes. Are we as careful about the moral shelter and sanitation which we provide in our homes?

Protection is not all. The lambs must be fed — not their bodies only, but their minds and their spiritual natures as well. Every home should provide for the best possible education of the children who come into it. The mother is the child's first teacher; her heart is the child's first schoolroom. The children should be taught early to look up to God, to trust him, to love and obey him. If they are Christ's lambs they should be trained from infancy to know their good Shepherd, to listen for his voice and to follow him.

The parents come first, but the teacher's part is also of the greatest importance in the shepherding of Christ's lambs. The Sunday school is the Church caring for the children. Very sacred are its functions. Its obligations cannot be met by any mere perfunctory or routine service. In the Jewish church the most urgent commands were given concerning the training of the children. They were to be instructed from their infancy in the holy Scriptures. These heavenly words were to be lodged in their hearts so early and so deeply that they would color their first thoughts, sweeten their first affections and give tone to all their aspirations and desires.

This is what we as teachers should seek to do for the young children in our classes. We should fill their hearts and minds with divine influences — the words which are able to make them wise unto salvation. We have the children when their lives are easily impressed, and when the blessing of our teaching will help to shape them for noble character and great usefulness. We should use the utmost diligence to take possession of them then for God.

Jesus made very clear the essential qualifications of a true shepherd. Before he committed his little lambs to the care of Peter,
he asked him in a most solemn way, "lovest
thou me?" and got his answer, "Yea, Lord."
There must be in the heart love for Christ, to
make the apostle ready to be a shepherd of
Christ's lambs. There was special reason why
the question should be pressed at this time.
Peter had sinned — he had said in his weakness that he was not one of the Master's
friends. He must unsay that denial and as-
sert his love for Christ in a most unmistakable way, before he could be intrusted with
the care of souls — little children's souls.

It is well that all who are set to care for
children should understand the full signifi-
cance of this requirement. Love for the
work itself is not enough. There are some
people who like to teach children, but this is
not a sufficient qualification. Enthusiasm
for children does not alone fit one for the
sacred work. The children are Christ's

especial care, and he will not intrust them to anyone who is not loyal to him, and who does not know him and love him.

He does not say that the shepherds must be very learned, or very wise, or highly cultured, but he does insist that they must love him. It is his work — caring for the children, and no one who does not feel toward them as Jesus himself does is ready to do the right work for them and in them. The lambs are tender and easily harmed. An ungentle touch would hurt them. An unkind word might mar the beauty of their spirit. Wrong advice might wreck their destiny.

It is evident that nothing but love will fit one to be a shepherd of Christ's lambs. Imagine a mother without affection. A little child is laid in her arms, but she does not love it. She undertakes the care of it in a perfunctory way, nursing it, providing for it, teaching and training it, yet all without love. Think of that tender young life growing up in this world of danger without the nurture of love! It might almost as well be in a home for foundlings as with an unloving mother.

But even the best human love, sweet and holy as it is, even mother love, the deepest, purest, most sacred of human affections, is not enough to prepare one to be a shepherd of the lambs. The love of Christ must be in the heart of one who would fittingly do this holy work. Unless a woman loves Christ — however she may love her child — she is not ready to be a true mother of little children who belong to Christ. The teacher who does not love Christ, however naturally affectionate and sympathetic she may be, lacks the essential qualification for being a true shepherd of Christ's little lambs.

Why is the love of Christ necessary for this shepherding? Nothing else in this world is so sensitive as a child's soul. A rough or careless touch may leave eternal marring on it. You go out one day with a geologist, and he shows you on certain rocks the prints of birds' feet, the indentations made by falling raindrops, the impression of a leaf with all its fine veinage marked. Once that rock was plastic clay, and the birds walked over it, the rain fell on it, and the leaf fluttered down and lay there. Next day the clay became dry and hardened, holding in it all these impressions. At length it became rock. Then some mighty upheaval tossed it to the side of a great mountain, where the man of science found it. But through all the long centuries, and in fire and flood, it has kept these ancient marks to tell the story of its origin.

Yet more sensitive to impressions than the plastic clay, and holding them yet more tenaciously, is the life of a little child. Every phase of influence that passes over it, even momentarily, leaves its own record indelibly written. If we who are caring for the gentle life are impatient, the impatience will leave its trace; if we grow angry, our anger will make a wound; if our life is impure, it will leave tarnishing. They must be holy, pure and meek, who would do Christ's work worthily on the soul of a little child. Nothing but the love of Christ in a heart will make it truly fit for the shepherding of Christ's lambs.

This wonderful love transforms the life in which it dwells. It makes the heart warm and tender; it makes one patient, thoughtful, kindly and sympathetic; it softens harshness and rudeness into gentleness; it gives one mercy and compassion toward the erring; it kindles that higher love which seeks the higher good of a life. When one loves Christ truly, one has some measure of Christ's own love, and is thus prepared to be as Christ to others.

We need to think seriously of the responsibility of taking a young life into our care for teaching and influence. There is a responsibility in all friendship. We are flattered when people come to us and wish to have us for friends. Confidence and love bring us pleasure. But what are you going to do with this new friend who has come into your life?

What kind of guardianship are you going to
exercise over him? Are you good enough to
take him under your influence?

One of Charles Lamb's letters gives a most
interesting illustration of unusual thoughtfulness in this line. A young person was dis-
posed to trust him as a friend, giving him his
confidence. Mr. Lamb wrote to this person
and said: "I do not wish to deter you from
making a friend, a true friend, and such
friendship, where the parties are not blind to
each other's faults, is very useful and valuable. I perceive a tendency in you to this
error. I know that you have chosen to take
up a high opinion of my moral worth, but, I
say it before God, and I do not lie, — you are
mistaken in me. I could not bear to lay open
all my failings to you, for the sentiment of
shame would be too pungent."

That was a brave and noble thing to do.
Not many men would have done it. Yet the
responsibility of accepting a new friend, especially when it is a child or a young person,

is always most serious. If our hands are not clean, if our hearts are not pure, if we are not ready to be absolutely true to the person, we dare not do it. Nothing but the love of Christ in the heart fits one to receive another life into the confidence and affection of holy friendship. It is a serious thing to take a class of children or young people, becoming their teacher; and if one has not the mind of the Master, one dare not do it. Before he intrusts his lambs for shepherding to any human care, Jesus asks with searching earnestness, "lovest thou me?" Then getting the answer, "Yea, Lord; thou knowest that I love thee," he says, "Feed my lambs."

When we love Christ truly, we are ready for any service he may give us, however sacred it may be. Then we can take the tender young life into our hands, and our touch will not harm it. Then we can answer the children's questions; for one who lives near the heart of Christ is taught of him, and can guide his little ones into the truth. Then the love of Christ, burning in us, will make us like Christ and just as we become like him are we ready to shepherd his little lambs.

CHAPTER II

THE TEACHER'S AIM

THE highest work given to mortals is that of winning souls. It is the work which Christ himself came into the world to do. His part was to reveal the love of God and then make redemption for lost men; the winning and gathering of perishing ones he committed to his disciples. In ordinary cases lost sinners are brought to repentance and faith only through those who already believe. There is only one Saviour, but human messengers must tell the story of his grace and bring men to him.

Christ does not go along the paths of life, seeking the lost, save in the persons of his disciples. The Holy Spirit does not, at least ordinarily, convict men of sin and lead them in penitence to the cross, by his immediate agency, but through the inspired Word, as spoken by cleansed human lips.

When we think of these truths, we see our great responsibility as Christians. Our mission in this world is to carry Christ to those who do not know him. This is especially true of all who as preachers and teachers are sent to present the gospel to others. They have a peculiar responsibility in this work. The Sunday-school teacher in whose heart there is not a strong desire to win souls has not yet realized the seriousness of the relation which he sustains to the members of his class. Those who sit before others with the Bible in their hands, to guide them into a knowledge of the truth, should make sure that they know their duty. The Holy Spirit desires through them to present Christ as Saviour and Lord. There are those who may never be saved unless it be through us; if we fail in our duty to them they may perish, and their blood will be upon us.

We have an illustration of the human part of salvation in our Lord's miracle of the loaves. The bread came from the Master's hands. The disciples themselves never could have fed the thousands with the little they happened to have. Yet neither did Jesus feed the multitude, save through his disciples. He gave the bread to them and they distributed it among the hungry ones who sat there on the green banks. The Master and his disciples were coworkers.

In this we see a picture of the manner in which the blessings of redemption reach lost men. Christ alone can prepare these blessings; no other one in the world could do this. He gave his own life to be bread for the hungry world. No other one can provide bread for our souls. Yet he does not with his own hands carry the bread to the perishing and hungry. He gives the loaves to his disciples and they pass them to the people.

But suppose those twelve men who were the mediators of the blessing of the bread that day had taken the loaves from the Master's hands, and, sitting down on the grass, had merely fed themselves, eating till they were satisfied, then laying down the bread, and not passing it to the hungry multitude waiting beyond them, what would have been the result? While there was bread enough to feed all the thousands, they would have remained unfed, because of the indolence and the selfishness of the disciples. The Master would have been balked in his purpose of mercy and compassion toward the people, not through any want of power in himself or of provision ready, but because his disciples had failed in their mission as distributors of the blessings which his hands had prepared.

The disciples did not act thus that day, however. Gladly and eagerly they carried the bread from group to group, till all the multitude was fed. But in the spiritual counterpart to that feeding, do the Lord's disciples never merely feed themselves, taking no thought for the hungry ones who are beyond them? They sit down at the gospel feast table and eat of the provisions that are offered, but do not think of the souls outside, who are perishing of hunger.

It is easy to see what terrible consequences may result from this neglect of duty. Souls may perish in their sins because we, in our thoughtlessness or in our spirit of self-indulgence, will not do our part by simply passing to them the bread of life. If we act thus we cannot say as Paul said, referring to the lost: "I am pure from the blood of all men."

It should always be a question with us, when we are interceding for others, asking blessing or help of any kind for them, whether it may not be our duty to take to them what we ask God to give them. There are times when to pray for one to be sent to do some work of Christ is less than useless — is even presumptuous. A city missionary, on his rounds, was passing a miserable hovel and heard cries as of children from within. He knocked but received no answer, the cries still continuing and indicating sore distress.

He opened the door and went in, and the spectacle that met his eyes was one to soften to tenderness the hardest heart. On a little heap of straw in one corner of the wretched apartment, lay a woman dead, and to her lifeless body two little children were clinging, weeping bitterly and calling to her. There was no fire and the room was cold.

The missionary was deeply touched by the pitiful sight, and his sympathy went out to the orphan children. He did not know what to do for them, and therefore fell upon his knees and prayed to God. He prayed unadvisedly, however, for he said: "O God, my faith this instant dies, unless thine open skies send help to these. Send some one — some angel, some messenger, to provide for them." But hardly had the words escaped his lips, when there came rebuke in answer to his rash thought. He seemed to hear, as if from the skies, the words: "Thou art my messenger — do not dare to leave my little ones. Lo, I have sent thee here for the very purpose of caring for them. To thy keeping this night I give them!"

So he arose and answered his own prayer. Giving a hand to each child, he led them away to shelter and care. Thus, many times, the only answer to our cries to God for help to others is, "Go thou, and minister to them in my name. Thou art my messenger."

When we ask how we may win souls, the answer is, that our part is that only of the messenger of Christ. When Jesus came down from the Mount of Transfiguration and the distressed father told him of his demoniac son, and how the disciples had tried in vain to cast out the demon, Jesus said, "Bring him hither to me." That is what he asks us always to do with the souls in whose salvation we are interested — "Bring them to me." That really is all we are to do — all we can do.

Yet there are some things to notice about the work of the messenger. Not everyone is ready to bring the lost to the Saviour. We must be vessels meet for the Master's use or he will not use us in this most sacred work.

For one thing, we must seek to make lost sinners know that God loves them. This really is the heart of the gospel message. It was to reveal this fact to men in their sins that the Son of God came down from heaven to earth. This is the message that he spoke in the ears of the weary, the lost, wherever he went. This was the gospel that shone out in his incarnate life as he moved about, — "God . . . manifested in the flesh." This was the meaning of the cross — it declared that God so loved the world that he gave his only begotten Son to be the world's Redeemer. This is the great burden of the message of the Church to men; it says to every sinner, "God loves you." He who really learns this one truth, whose heart learns it, and who can say in the glow of happy consciousness, "God loves me," is saved. The first thing, therefore, in those who sit down before others to try to win them, is to make it plain and clear to them that God loves them.

For another thing, there should be in the teacher's own heart a genuine love for souls, a true compassion for the unsaved. Some measure of the love that brought Christ from heaven to earth, and led him to his wonderful condescension and sacrifice, we must have, if we would be his messengers in bringing others to him. If we would be soul winners, we must have the mind that was in Christ Jesus. Until we have in us something of this compassion, it is scarcely worth our while to try to lead souls to the Saviour. "God loves you and I love you," was the message of Mr. McAll to the people of Paris, when he first began his work among them. There is little use in our telling people the first part of this message if we cannot tell them also the second part of it. We must love or we cannot tell of God's love. The love of Christ must throb in our hearts, shine in our faces, melt in our eyes, tremble in our words, and offer itself again on the cross in our lives, if we would win souls to heaven.

There is a practical suggestion in the scriptural word: "He that is wise winneth souls." Souls cannot be driven to Christ, they cannot be coerced into discipleship; they must be won. When we study the manner of Christ among men, we readily see how he sought to save the lost. He loved people into his kingdom. He proved himself the Friend of sinners. He sought not to be "ministered unto, but to minister." He loved to do good to others, to help them, to comfort them. Grace shone in his face and in his whole life.

If we would bring souls to Christ we must win them. The teacher who is cold in his manner may teach earnestly and evangelically, but he will not gain souls for his Master. It is the teacher that has a warm heart, and whose heart melts into his words and his life, who will be most greatly blessed in his work. We can win others for Christ and save them, only by love.

The first bringing of pupils to Christ is not the whole of the teacher's work. They are then to be watched over with new care, wisely guided, faithfully shepherded, helped in all true ways, built up into strength and led out into fields of active service. To this sacred ministry every teacher is called and ordained. Fulfilling his ministry with faithful earnestness, he will shine as the stars forever and ever.

CHAPTER III

PREPARATION is more than half; indeed, in many things, it is nearly all. Work for which preparation has not been well made is scarcely worth while. One who expects to make anything noble of his chosen calling, prepares for it with great diligence and painstaking. Men serve a long apprenticeship to be ready to do the work of their trade. Inadequate preparation results in incompetent workmanship, and that foredooms one to failure. No man can hope to succeed in business without a business training which will enable him to grapple with the problems of trade. No one can rise to distinction in a profession without laborious study and self-discipline. Most of the failures in life may be traced directly to the lack of thorough preparation. Men are in haste to get into the field and do not take time to fit themselves for the responsibilities and duties which await them.

What is true in general of all callings and pursuits is yet more true of work on mind and heart; most careful preparation should be made for it. Before a man is considered competent to be a physician, to be intrusted with the treatment of diseases and the performance of critical surgical operations, he must undergo a training of years under the best instructors. Can it be any less responsible work to be a physician of souls, — to be a teacher, for example, of a class of children or young people in a Sunday school?

We do not realize the criticalness of the work we have to do when we sit down beside another to talk with him of spiritual things. His eternal destiny may depend on what we say to him in that very lesson. He may be at one of the turning points of his life, at the parting of the ways; and when we have taught our lesson the decision may have been made. It is always most serious work to teach others in spiritual things. We need wise and thorough preparation for it.

It is a fearful thing to do any work carelessly. Careless carpentering may result in insecurity in a building in which men and women are to live; and disaster may result. Careless casting may lead to the putting of a flawed beam into the great bridge, and one night in the darkness a train filled with sleeping passengers is hurled into the waters to perish. Careless plumbing may result in typhoid fever or diphtheria. Carelessness in any kind of work leaves danger behind it. But negligence in spiritual work, in work for souls, may lead to the most far-reaching evil consequences. Those who would do the Lord's work need the most careful training for it.

Two kinds of preparation are necessary. One is general, bearing upon the life and character of the teacher and running through many years. This preparation begins with personal devotement to Christ. This must always be first. We must come to Christ before we can go forth for Christ. We must be Christians before we are teachers. The Twelve were appointed "that they might be with him," and that, when they were trained, he "might send them forth." We are not ready to be intrusted with the care of souls until our own soul is saved and we are following Christ.

Preparation for teaching includes also personal knowledge of Christ. It is not enough to know about him — we must know him. Teaching never can be effective which is only a retelling of what some other one has said. That was the weakness of the teaching of the scribes in our Lord's day. They quoted what the rabbis had said. We must be able to tell what we ourselves know. Personal friendship with Christ is a necessary qualification for one who would be a teacher in the school of Christ.

Another element of preparation is familiarity with the Scriptures. Of course, the

Bible is such a vast treasure house that even a lifetime spent in researches in it cannot exhaust it; hence it cannot be said that one must know all about the Bible before he is prepared to be a teacher. One may begin with very little knowledge and yet be an efficient teacher, but he must be a diligent student of the Word, meanwhile, and all the while.

Another element of preparation in a teacher is his own heart life. Miss Havergal used to say that a great deal of living must go to a very little writing. It is quite as true that a great deal of living must go to a very little teaching. Really, we can teach only what we have learned by experience. When the minister said he had been thirty years preparing the sermon which he had just delivered with such power, he spoke truly, although, perhaps, the immediate preparation of the discourse had required but a few hours. Thirty years' life, with its experiences, had gone into the sermon. Any sermon or lesson is valuable just in proportion to the amount of life that has entered into it.

Another element in personal preparation must be made in the teacher's character. If he is not a good man he is not fit to touch the souls of others. He should live so carefully and conscientiously that he will never be afraid to look any man in the face. He needs the preparation of attested character. His neighbors must be able to witness well for him. A doubtful reputation disqualifies one for effective teaching. The good work he may do through his lessons on Sundays will be neutralized by the influence of his life on week days.

One of our Lord's most suggestive teachings is against hiding one's light under a bushel. Our spiritual life is a lamp burning in the heart and we are to make our character so crystalline and keep so clean that the shining will never be obscured. Any inconsistency in conduct will dim something of the brightness of the light. Anything that is not Christlike in our behavior or disposition will hinder the full, free shining out of the light within us. A beautiful life is a noble preparation for teaching. Those who sit before classes on Sunday should have white souls and untarnished names.

So much for the teacher's general preparation, the preparation which comes through Christian nurture. This is put first, because it is first in value and importance. One may be a successful teacher without being great among men or even without being a great theologian; but one never can leave deep, heavenly impressions on other lives without being good. One must have clean hands in order to put touches of beauty on immortal lives.

But there is also a specific and definite preparation which every teacher needs to make. The lesson must be prepared. To a young minister who was in danger of trusting too much to mere glowing ardor to the neglect of painstaking preparation, an old minister wrote, "You are quite right to trust God with your work; but remember that it was beaten incense that was used for the service of the sanctuary." Love for Christ does not preclude the necessity for hard study, either in a minister or in a teacher. Back of the class work on Sundays should always be as many hours as the teacher can get during the week for the careful study of the lesson. It is wonderful, too, how much time even the busiest teacher can get by using merely the fragments of time that most people waste. Twenty minutes daily will make two whole hours in a week.

This is not the place to speak of the way to prepare a lesson, further than to say that it must be conscientiously done. No slovenly work will either please God or leave good results in the life and character of a pupil. We are builders. Paul loves to use the word "edify" of those who are engaged in Christian work. In one remarkable passage he speaks of two kinds of building materials which may be used even by good men, working, too, on the true foundation. One may build into the wall, wood, hay and stubble, or gold, silver and costly stones. The illustration is very suggestive, and never was the caution as to what we should build into others' life-temples more needed than in these very days. There are countless materials ever close to our hand which we might use, which would be only wood, hay and stubble in the fabric.

It is easy to understand the consequences of carelessness or unfaithfulness in deciding what to give our pupils when we sit before them. To teach falsehood is to build into their lives that which will leave eternal marring. To teach mere trivial things, bits of sentiment, idle fancies, is to build wood, hay and stubble into the wall, amid the gold, silver and precious stones. The illustration suggests the unfitness of such materials in a temple in which every smallest fragment should be rich in its beauty and worth. In preparing our lessons we should take exceeding care that nothing unworthy shall ever be brought to give to the eager spirits that wait for us every Sunday. Nothing but truth is fit to build in the house we are rearing for God.

In all his preparation the teacher should work for the eye of God, never for man's eye. He should do just as carefully and painstakingly the things which only God shall see, as the things which human eyes may see and human lips commend and praise. An English dealer, interviewing Oka, the great modern Japanese carver of ivories, said to him: "Why do you waste your time in carving the under part which is never seen? You could work much quicker and make money far more rapidly if you were to leave that part plain." The carver answered, "God who gave me skill and taste, can see the under part; I dare not leave it uncarved." That is the spirit in which the work is done in Japan. Small wonder that it excels in beauty and individuality!

Really all our work is for the eye of God.
That which men never will see, God sees.
We dare do nothing negligently, for we are
doing our most obscure taskwork for the
great Master's eye. Those who are to open
God's Word on Sundays, interpreting to a
class of children or young people the meaning of a passage of Holy Scriptures, should
make most diligent preparation in patient,
quiet study, so that they may give no mistaken instruction and that the teaching
may be interesting and impressive.

It has been said that the words "That will
do" have done more harm than any other
sentence in the English language. Too many
Sunday-school teachers let this motto of easy-
going indolence rule them in their preparation of their lessons. They fail to realize
the serious nature of the work they are set to
do. They feel that anything will do for a
class of boys or girls, forgetting that these
young minds are most impressible and these
young hearts open to influences which will

shape their whole future. Nothing but the most careful and most thorough preparation the teacher can possibly give to his lesson during the week is worthy of the sacredness of his work or will satisfy the Master.

There is also a devotional preparation which every teacher should make before going to his class. He should go from the presence of God to his place of duty. Then his own heart will be set on fire at the flame of God's altar, and, looking into the face of Christ, he will receive his commission for the work before him. Laying all his preparation at the Master's feet, the blessing of the Holy Spirit will come upon it, and he will be a man indeed sent from God, a prophet, to speak the words of God to those whom he shall find waiting to listen to him. With such preparation as this, no teacher can ever fail in the work to which he has devoted himself.

CHAPTER IV

THE SPIRITUAL ELEMENT IN TEACHING

MANY factors enter into successful Sunday-school teaching. A good building is desirable. No doubt good Bible study has been secured in dark basements. No doubt good teaching can be done in a barn; but all will admit that an ideal Sunday-school building is of great value in the making of an ideal school.

Good scientific teaching is also desirable. It would certainly be the ideal way to have all Sunday-school teachers trained as public school-teachers are now trained, not only in thorough knowledge of the things which they are to teach, but also in methods of teaching, so that they could give instruction in a scientific way. The time has gone by when piety will serve as a teacher's only qualification.

Careful and painstaking preparation is also

important. It will not do to neglect the study of the lesson through the week, and then expect the Holy Spirit to help one to teach effectively, intelligently and impressively, when one comes into the presence of a class. Prayer is mighty, but prayer will not bring into the life either gifts or graces for which we have been too indolent to toil.

Then, in emphasizing the spiritual element in teaching, there must be no disparagement of the value of the Bible words and facts which make up the body of the lessons. It is not suggested that the teacher should neglect the inspired text and spend his time in pious moralizing. Nor is he to substitute in place of such Scriptural matters, stories of his own, however touching and appealing they may be, supposing that in this way he can better reach the hearts of his pupils than by opening up to their minds the words of God.

Nor will it do to despise the geography, the ethnography, the biography, the meteorology, the history, of the Bible. Some teachers think they must omit all such matters as these and dwell only upon purely spiritual things. But this is very superficial and ineffective teaching. The Bible is a book of facts. The Old Testament is chiefly a history of God's chosen people from Abraham to Malachi. Then the New Testament is chiefly a history of the life, work, death and resurrection of Jesus Christ, and the beginning of the Church, with a handful of old letters written by apostles to different churches and persons. Nothing is too small to be noticed.

We should try as teachers to become thoroughly familiar with every statement, to know the meaning of every allusion. Then we should not regard our work with our pupils as well done if we have failed to make plain and.clear to them the facts which form the framework of the lesson we are set to teach. One of the aims of every Sunday-school teacher should be to know the Bible well as a book, to become conversant with its contents — its histories, its persons, its incidents, its allusions. Then, teaching will be intelligent, misinterpretation will be less frequent, and the Word of God will indeed make men wise unto salvation.

Yet there is always need to emphasize the spiritual element in Sunday-school teaching. Recently there was published an account of a visit of an American to the Jewish schools and synagogues in the ancient city of Bagdad. The visitor was shown to the room where convened the highest court of the Jewish community. On a dais sat, in oriental fashion, five old men who were expounding the law to any who had questions of duty to propound to them. The guide called the visitor's attention to the venerable, white-bearded rabbi in the center of this group, and said, "That is the most learned scholar of the Talmud in the world." "But," said the visitor, "we think we have some very learned rabbis in our country." "So you have," replied the guide, "but they study the Talmud as a science, while we study it as a religion."

This answer suggests two ways of studying the Bible—as a science and as a religion. It may be studied only as literature; or it may be studied also as a book of religion, to learn from it its revealings of God, and its teaching concerning human duty. The first is not to be neglected, but the second is the vital thing, that without which no Sunday-school teaching is complete or satisfactory.

A visitor to Westminster Abbey once heard a celebrated dean preach on the parable of the Good Samaritan. The sermon was brilliant and scholarly, and described with great vividness the scenes through which the traveler passed as he went his way. The visitor wrote to one of his friends, however, that he had learned a great deal about the way from Jerusalem to Jericho, but nothing of the way through earth to heaven.

The criticism may have been too severe,

and yet it suggests a danger in all Bible
teaching against which we need ever to be on
our guard. We can readily imagine a teacher
devoting the whole of the thirty or forty
minutes of the lesson time to the facts and
incidents of the passage assigned for study,
with not a minute for any spiritual instruction. Evidently this would not fulfill the
true purpose of Sunday-school instruction.

What is the object at which teaching should
always aim? For one thing, it should be to
make the pupils acquainted with the Bible
as a book. But this is not the only aim.
The Bible is given, primarily, to reveal to us
the character and the will of God, and then
to show us human need and the way of
salvation. It is meant to guide us through
this world to our Father's house. When we
sit down before a class of children or young
people, evidently our first duty is to tell them
what the Word of God means for them.
Failing in this, however well we may have
taught the lesson, we have failed to teach the

part of the lesson which we were appointed
specially to make plain and clear to them.
The messages of the Bible are personal and
individual; if the pupil gets no word for
himself, going straight to his heart, the
teaching has not reached its highest mission.

One day a primary class teacher was putting on a blackboard the golden text of the
lesson. It was, "Christ Jesus came into
the world to save sinners."

When she had finished, one of the little
ones said, "O teacher, you have left out
Jesus." She looked, — the child was right.
Too often the teacher leaves out Jesus in his
teaching.

This suggests the importance of the
practical and personal application of the
lesson. What is the bearing of this portion
of God's Word on the common, everyday
life of our pupils? When we stand before our
classes on Sunday, we must so interpret to
them the words of the Scriptures we are
studying that its heavenly light shall be cast

upon their path on Monday and Tuesday. We may think of their life as it must be lived for six week days. Or perhaps we look back over the past week. Some of them have had sorrow. One has been sick, and is out again for the first time. One has come from an unhappy home. They all have had their struggles and some of them have been hurt in the week's life. We must so teach our lesson in the thirty minutes, that every hungry, craving heart before us shall receive something, that not one of them shall go away unfed.

We must not fail to bring out the great facts of the lesson; but we must find also for our class the word of God that lies in these facts like a grain of gold in the quartz. We must get the word for the sorrowing heart, for the one who is carrying the heavy burden, for the one who is pale from illness, for the one who has been hurt in the week's struggle, for the one whose home is not happy or does not help him heavenward. We must find a message of cheer for the discouraged one, a word of hope for the one who is almost despairing, and a word of warning for the careless one. Then we must put into each heart a thought of courage which will make it braver and stronger for another stretch of life till the Sabbath comes again.

We must try to make God real to our pupils, so that they may go forth conscious of his being, of his interest in them and his love for them. We must try to help them to realize the presence of Christ and to become conscious of his friendship. Then we must make them feel a sense of their own responsibility for life — that for another week they must go out to live purely, sweetly, joyfully, unselfishly, helpfully. They must get inspiration from our lesson to help them to live with energy and hope, and with fear of God and love for men in their heart, for a whole new week of very real experience. We have our pupils for only one hour, but in that hour we should strive to put into their hearts impulses and inspirations which will make them live better, and work at their tasks more faithfully, until the Sabbath comes again.

Much of the teacher's power in spiritual work must lie in his own personality. Personality is the force at the heart of a man which gives energy, which drives the machinery of his life, which determines character. It is what a man is that gives force and value to what he says and does. There are some people whose personality is so charming that it imparts a subtle influence to every common word they speak and the most trivial thing they do.

The teacher's personality is a most potent factor in his teaching. There are teachers, — scholarly, well-trained, who teach scientifically, and pour on every lesson a flood of wisdom, yet who cannot keep a class together. Pupils will not stay with them. They have no attractive power. There are other teachers who have not one tenth of the

teaching ability of these, and yet they hold
pupils close about them, win their affection
and confidence, and teach them lessons which
make good Christians of them and prepare
them for noble life. The secret lies in their
personality — they are spiritually-minded.
They have the love of Christ in them, and
this love fills all their being and sweetens all
their life.

Few things are sadder than the mistakes
made by some good people in their endeavor
to teach religion. They show at least ordinary common sense in other matters, but the
moment they begin to speak of Christ and
religion all their naturalness forsakes them
and they assume a tone of voice they never
use when speaking on any other topic. They
wear a long face, as if being a Christian were
the saddest thing in the world. The whole
manner of their treatment of the subject is
such that happy, wholesome young persons
are repelled. How much better it would be
if in all our presentations of religion we

should make it bright, sunny and attractive, so that the young may learn to think of being a Christian as the sweetest, truest, loveliest life possible to them. Spirituality does not mean solemnity. Piety is not something gloomy and forbidding. Being good is not being long faced. The ideal teacher should be full of sunshine and his speech full of song and cheer.

CHAPTER V

L IVING must always go before teaching and must enforce it. Personal character is that which gives value and weight to our speech. We all know men who talk eloquently and say excellent things, but whose words have little influence. The reason is that their life, as men see it, fails to give evidence of sincerity and earnestness. Then we know other men whose words are plain, perhaps who falter and stumble in speech, but whose lives are so true and so evidently Spirit-filled, that their simplest sentences have weight and influence.

Other things are important. A teacher should be intelligent; inaccuracies of statement make marring and confusion in the minds of the pupils. He should not fail to be thoroughly familiar with the Scriptures which he is to expound, so that error in fact or in doctrine may never be taught by him. Wrong teaching in spiritual things may wreck a destiny. Aptness to teach is also an important qualification in one who undertakes to instruct others. There are many persons of large intelligence, whose knowledge of the subject concerning which they are to teach is full and accurate, but who yet lack the teaching faculty. A Bible teacher should be apt to teach.

Yet, while all these and other qualifications are essential, that which after all counts for most in the teacher is the element of personal character. Nothing but heart can reach and impress heart. It is life alone that can quicken and nourish life. It is the man as he is that gives influence and force to what the teacher says and does. It was Arnold the man quite as much as Arnold the teacher who did such important service for English boys at Rugby. The same is true of everyone who does effective and enduring work in school and class. This is especially true in Sunday-school teaching, where the lessons to be taught are moral and spiritual, having for their object the building up of character. The best teachers, measured by scientific standards, will fail altogether of real effectiveness if their teaching be not enforced and sustained by a good and worthy character.

It goes without saying that inconsistency in the life and conduct of a teacher vitiates, perhaps altogether annuls, the best and wisest instruction. We must not only point out the right way to those who sit before us to be taught and guided, but must ourselves walk in the way. Christ came in the flesh to bring the life of God down close enough to us for us to see it, and we in turn as teachers are to bring down in our own personality the life of Christ, close to those whom we would help, so that they also will follow Christ.

That was Paul's way of teaching, — "I beseech you therefore, be ye imitators of me." He was to men the interpreter of Christ. He invited people to look at him to see in his life a miniature of Christ's. "Be ye imitators of me, even as I also am of Christ." He was not afraid to ask those he taught to take him as their example. Nor in this confidence did he take any honor from Christ. He was conscious in his heart that he was following Christ, and showing in his own life and character the fruits of the Spirit which he desired to see in others.

Every teacher should have the same consciousness; he should make sure that if his pupils imitate him they will also imitate Christ. A little child came to her mother with this question: "Is Jesus like anybody I know?" She was trying to make out in her own thought what Jesus was like. Her mother should have been able to say: "Yes, I am trying to be like Jesus — I am a little like him. Look at me, and you will learn what he is like." It requires a high order of Christian living to give one this confidence, but those who represent Christ as teachers should live near the Master, and should be so blameless in their character that they need not fear men's eyes. They should be able to say what Paul said.

How can we who are older and have more experience expect those younger than ourselves, who wait on us for pattern and guidance, to try to live better than we are living? We can teach only what we know, and we really know of Christ only what we get wrought into conduct and character, into act and disposition. We can lead others only over paths that are familiar to our own feet. We are called to be witnesses of Christ, and a witness is not a repeater merely of something he has heard; he can tell only what he has seen and learned by personal observation and experience. No one can ever teach more of Christ than he knows through acquaintance and personal friendship with Christ. All efforts, therefore, to guide others further into spiritual life than we have gone ourselves, are futile and unavailing.

However glibly the words may fall from

our lips, there is no power in that teaching which has cost us nothing more than a little conning or memorizing of sentences. The lessons which impress others as we speak them must come out of our own heart, and must have been fused in the alembic of our own experience. We must have learned them for ourselves, perhaps in struggle and pain, or our most eloquent counsels and exhortations will have no more warmth in them than winter sunbeams dancing among icicles. Indeed, teaching with which our own daily life and conduct do not harmonize inspires only sneers in those who listen to us. It does only harm to the cause we would advance.

Nothing comes of an irascible, quick-tempered man's moralizing on the duty of gentleness and sweetness of disposition. There is no use in a close, hard, exacting, miserly man commending the Master's teaching, "It is more blessed to give than to receive," for his conduct shows that he does not really believe what he commends. One who

is known to be untruthful will have little
influence in urging ever so eloquently the
duty of truthfulness. An uncharitable and
resentful man cannot effectively inculcate
the lessons of charity and forgiveness, for he
himself has never learned the lessons. Children are very soon old enough to detect
inconsistency in life and conduct in those
who, by accepting the place of teachers, say
to them in effect, "Be ye imitators of me,
even as I also am of Christ," while they so
distinctly fail to live as Christ lived. It is
only when the teaching grows out of the
living that it has power over others.

On the other hand, beautiful character
always impresses itself on other lives. It is
like a gospel which silently and continuously
preaches its own evangel. Simple goodness
in a teacher has an influence over young lives,
like that which summer skies have over
fields and forests. It inspires, quickens and
woos out the best things in mind and heart.
The secret is the indwelling of the divine

Spirit in the heart that is truly consecrated to God. The outcome of such inner life is Christlike character.

Those who work in clay or in paints or chemicals, in flour mills or in coal mines, carry with them from their work into the streets the marks of their occupation. We know, when we meet them, where they have been, and what they have been doing. We know, when we observe men's manners, and hear their speech, whether they are educated or untaught, refined or rude. In like manner those who have been with Jesus carry out from his presence the unmistakable marks of communion with him. All who meet them feel in their every word and act, in their very silent presence, the influence of the power that is in them; and there is no other power that is so effective in impressing life. One who lives near to God is struck through, as it were, with the life and the Spirit of God. His very face is transfigured, as the inner light shines out through his features. His simplest sentences have an unction that makes them impressive. His presence is a benediction wherever he goes.

Every Sunday-school teacher should seek to possess spiritual power. He can find it by living near to God. Those who commune with God will come from their closets to their classes like Moses from the forty days on the mount, their faces shining with the brightness of God's holy love. Communion with God must always go before good service. There can be no largely useful life which is not inspired by fellowship with Christ. There is no other secret of spiritual power. Nothing can work the works of God but God himself in the heart. There can be no mere imitation here. No set of rules can be prescribed, the following of which will produce certain spiritual results. Power in Christian work can come only through Christ living in us.

It is a serious responsibility which one accepts who becomes a teacher of the young; it is a perilous thing for a teacher to occupy a

place in the presence of all the possibilities
that lie in young lives, and then to be un-
faithful or even negligent. It is a serious
thing if, being helpful in many ways, the
teacher yet fails in the higher spiritual work
which belongs to one who is set as a guide
to human souls. We may do many good
things for our pupils who gather about us and
look into our face; we may teach them many
things that will adorn their life and character;
we may impart to them knowledge that will
be of value to them in their life and work;
we may aid them in other ways — in literature, in social life, in their general culture;
yet, if we do not succeed in leading them to
Christ, and fashioning in them the divine
likeness, we have failed in that part of our
duty and responsibility which is most essential and vital, that without which all our help
avails not in the end. Few words are sadder,
when all the facts of her life are considered,
than these lines by the gifted and brilliant
H. H., — the last she ever wrote, telling of

her want of satisfaction with her life work
when she came to consider it, when facing the
facts of eternity:

> Father, I scarcely dare to pray,
>   So clear I see now it is done,
> That I have wasted half my day,
>   And left my work but just begun.
>
> So clear I see that things I thought
>   Were right or harmless were a sin;
> So clear I see that I have sought,
>   Unconscious, selfish aim to win;
>
> So clear I see that I have hurt
>   The souls I might have helped to save,
> That I have slothful been, inert,
>   Deaf to the calls thy leaders gave.
>
> In outskirts of thy kingdom vast,
>   Father, the humblest spot give me;
> Set me the lowest task thou hast,
>   Let me repentant, work for thee!

A teacher needs to be most watchful and
faithful, not only with his teaching, but also
in his personal life, that from the end of it all,
when he faces eternity, he may not have to
look back with tears of repentance over a
failure. Of all the solemn sayings of Jesus,

none are more solemn than his words concerning him who should cause one of his little ones to stumble. "It is profitable for him that a great millstone should be hanged about his neck, and that he should be sunk in the depth of the sea." We need the mind of Christ in us, the gentleness of Christ, the patience of Christ, the thoughtfulness of Christ, that we may never misguide a child that asks us the way home; and we need to be filled with the grace of Christ, flowing out in conduct, disposition, and character, so that never by any act, word, or influence of ours, we may cause a little one to stumble, hurting a soul we might have helped to save.

CHAPTER VI

THE TEACHER REPRESENTING CHRIST

IT is a great advantage to have clear and
definite thoughts of duty. Many persons seem never to have any very serious
views of life. They do not know for what
purpose they are in this world, what their
mission is. Indeed they never give any
earnest thought to the matter. They appear
to have no conception of the responsibility
of being in this world.

Many live as if there were neither God nor
man nor Devil, as if there were neither moral
law, nor human accountability, nor divine
judgment. But too many others who even
call themselves Christians and who recite
their creed on every opportunity, seem also
to live almost as indifferently as these. They
have no thought of their relation to the
kingdom of Christ, of their place as redeemed

ones, belonging to God, or of their duty as Christians to do Christ's work in the world.

Not many even godly Christians seem to understand their personal responsibility as coworkers with God, as helpers of Christ in saving the world. It is important that those at least who as teachers are earnestly desirous of doing their part in guiding others, should have a clear conception of what they are to do and how they are to do it.

The mission of Christians in this world was very clearly defined by the great Teacher, when he said to his disciples, "As the Father hath sent me, even so send I you." That is, we bear the same relation to Christ that he bore to the Father. He was sent by the Father and we are sent by Christ. What a dignity, a sacredness, a seriousness it gives to our life, to remember that we are sent from Christ and for him! We are not in the world in any mere haphazard way, or on any mere chance errand; we are sent from God. It follows that we represent him who sent us;

we are his ambassadors; we speak for him. This is true not only of ministers, those who are ordained to the holy office; it is true of every Christian, and especially of those who are called to teach others the truths of divine revelation.

Our mission, too, is the same as was that of Christ. He was called the Word. A word reveals thoughts. Our friend stands before us silent, and we know not what is in his heart. Then he speaks, and his words tell us what his feelings are. The world could not know the thoughts that were in the heart of God. No man could go up to heaven to see God. Then God sent his Son — the Word — to reveal his thoughts, and men learned that God is their Father, with a father's love, care, tenderness, compassion. They learned also the divine mercy and grace. For three years Jesus went about speaking in human language great thoughts about God and showing in his life the dispositions, affections, feelings, and character of God. We, too, in our little way, are to be words of God, revealing what is in the divine heart. As Jesus said, "He that hath seen me hath seen the Father," we should be able to say, "He that hath seen me hath seen Christ."

This teaching puts upon us a sacred responsibility. Wherever we go we must be as Christ. Christ is no more here in his own humanity — we are now the body of Christ. He does not go about doing good, but we are to go about and do what he would do if he were here again. We are to be Christ to others, and we need to watch our life, lest sometimes we misrepresent him. We should never give a wrong interpretation of any thought, feeling or spirit of Christ.

It is part of our work as Christians to do the work of Christ. For three years he went up and down the land, speaking the words of God, doing the works of God. Those were wonderful days. Then he died on a cross. How he must have been missed when he came no more to the people's homes! What a blessing his ministry had been, with its miracles of healing and its common kindnesses which cheered and brightened so many lives! The world needed just such love amid its want, pain and sorrow. How much poorer this earth seemed when it was known that Jesus was dead, that he would go among the sick and troubled no more! What a pity it seemed that such a ministry should cease!

Yet it did not cease. Jesus went away himself, but he had trained his disciples to do the gentle things he himself had been doing for three years, and now sent them out to continue the ministry. It is the mission of Christ's followers, wherever they are, to do the things that Jesus would do if he were here. We cannot perform miracles, but we may do many Christly things. His love should ever be in our hearts, revealing itself in whatever forms of helpfulness the human needs about us may require.

"Is your father at home?" a gentleman

asked a child, on the village doctor's door-
step.

"No, sir," the boy answered; "he's away."

"Where do you think I could find him?"

"Well, you've got to look for him some
place where people are sick, or hurt, or something like that. I do not know where he is,
but he's helping somewhere."

If one had been seeking for Jesus in Galilee,
he would have found him where people were
sick or distressed in some way. He was
always helping somewhere. By the same
mark his disciples should be known in any
community. They should always be helping
some one, comforting sorrow, giving cheer,
encouragement, strength. Thus the ministry
begun by Christ, nineteen hundred years ago,
in the little country of Palestine, should go
on wherever the followers of Christ are found.

Especially should those who are set to be
teachers of others in spiritual things, carry
out this part of the Master's commission.

They represent Christ and it is not enough

that they tell in words the meaning of Christ's gospel; they should also, in their own lives, truly and faithfully represent Christ as a minister of good, a giver of help, a dispenser of blessing.

It is part of the mission of Christians also to help Christ to save the world. He was sent to redeem the lost. He gave his life in service of love to lift up the fallen. We are exhorted to have the mind in us which was also in Christ Jesus — the love which brought him from glory. We are not sent as he was to die on the cross; one atonement was sufficient. Yet we are to have the same love for the lost that he had. Instead of taking us to a cross it should lead us into a life consecrated to the saving of the world. We never can be as Christ was in the world, and continue to live for ourselves. Service is the key word of the Christ-life service, even to sacrifice. We must lay down our lives in love, whether it be in living or dying.

These are hints of the meaning of the words

of Christ when he said that as the Father had sent him, so he sends us. What he was to the people among whom he went in his large way as the Son of God, we are to be to those among whom we move in our small way as his followers. We are his apostles as he was the Father's Apostle. We are to reveal him in our lives as he in his life revealed the Father. We are to continue the ministry of love which he began. We are to give ourselves for the world as he gave himself on Calvary.

All this may seem discouraging. The responsibility of representing Christ and being to the world in any measure what he was, may appear to be too vast to be met by any human soul. But there was something else which Jesus said which makes us ready to take up our burden. Immediately after defining the relation of his disciples to him and to the world, he breathed on them and said, "Receive ye the Holy Spirit." Without this divine enduement they never could have

been in the world what he had been. The
Holy Spirit is in one sense the same as Christ
returned to earth. Instead of living now in
one human body he lives in every believer.
Thus he is really continuing his own ministry
in his people. The love that is in us is but
the love of Christ beating in our heart.
The holiness that we attain is but the holiness of Christ reproducing itself in our lives.
The beautiful things that appear in our
characters — love, joy, peace, long-suffering,
meekness — are but the graces of Christ
wrought in us by his own indwelling — the
fruits of the Spirit, as Paul calls them.

We never can have these qualities in us
unless we receive the Holy Spirit. No mere
human culture can produce them. They are
fruits which do not grow on the stalk of
nature. We can do the works of God only if
God be in us. But that is what it is to be a
Christian. "Christ liveth in me," is Paul's
description of himself as a believer. There
is no other true definition.

How can we receive the Holy Spirit and thus have the divine life in us? The word "receive" answers the question. The Spirit never will be forced upon us; we must receive him. It requires an act of our own. We can shut him out of our lives if we will. In receiving the Spirit we must surrender every thing to him. He must be admitted to rule, to guide, to sway all the life.

An old Dutch picture shows a little child dropping a cherished toy out of his hand. At first one does not understand why he does this, but closer observation shows, at an upper corner of the picture, a white dove which is flying toward the empty, outstretched hands. The child has dropped the toy to receive the dove.

Ofttimes our hands clutch things which are dear, things which we have toiled hard to gain. But there is something better, — "Receive ye the Holy Spirit" are the words that fall from the lips of Christ. Shall we not gladly drop out of our hands any possessions, any pleasures, anything, in order that we may receive the dove of peace?

People talk about having to give up so much to become Christians; but do they give up much? Or is the giving up to be compared with the receiving? Is the man making a sacrifice who drops his wood, hay and stubble, to take gold, silver and precious stones? Shall we talk of giving up, when we let go our toys and glittering trifles, to receive the Holy Spirit? Were the first disciples losers when they left their nets and boats and homes and went after Christ, to find homelessness, persecution and martyrdom? It seemed a loss but they dropped out of their hands only a few poor, perishable things, to receive imperishable riches, honors and glories.

We should never hesitate, therefore, to yield our lives to the Holy Spirit, whatever emptying of our hands it must take to prepare the way. To receive the Spirit is to let God take us, that he may bless us and use us in being as Christ to a weary, suffering and sinning world.

Those who would lead others into complete surrender, into fullness of blessing, into nobleness of confession, themselves need all the fullness of God, that they may truly represent the Master in the world.

CHAPTER VII

THE TEACHER'S SPIRITUAL CULTURE

THE word culture is used first of land —
the act of tilling and preparing it for
fertility. The ground is cultivated in order
to make it yield the best harvests. The
word is applied also to the act of promoting
growth in plants, especially with a view to the
improvement of their quality and the produc-
tion of new varieties. It is wonderful what
results are obtained in flowers, for example,
by culture.

The word is used also of the improvement
of the mind and the refinement of the character, under the influence of education. It
is not only the acquiring of knowledge, the
becoming familiar, for example, with literature, that is meant; it includes also the effect
on the life, the thoughts, the feelings, of
familiar contact with refinement. We all
know the influence on the nature of intimate

association with those who are intelligent and refined.

There is also a spiritual culture, the improving, enriching and refining of the spiritual part of our being. We begin our Christian life as children, in the lowest forms at school. Yet we are to grow in all the qualities which belong to beautiful Christian character. Spiritual culture is the process by which our nature is softened and mellowed into the gentleness of love, our talents are developed into their best possibilities of usefulness, and our whole life is transformed into the beauty of Christ.

It is very important that those who teach others should themselves have a rich spiritual culture. We cannot impart what we do not possess. The influence of one's personality is among the most potent influences in one's life. Manners are far more important than we are apt to suppose. Our smallest rudenesses are as dead flies in the perfumer's ointment, which mar its sweetness. Refinement is in itself not only a charm but a subtle power in one's personality. There is a spiritual refinement in some people which adds manifold to the value of all they do or say. It is indefinable. We cannot analyze it nor tell what its secret is, but it is an unmistakable power. Everyone who would guide others in spiritual things should seek for this charm of spiritual culture.

We should long for the best that we can attain. The Master would have all his servants vigorous and wholesome Christians. He desires not only that they may have life, but that they may have abundant life. He always expects large things from faith and consecration. He spoke of the new life he gives as a well of living water in the heart, and said that from this fountain, not a trickling streamlet but rivers of water, shall flow. It should be our aim to attain the high standard that the Master has set for us. We should be content with nothing less than the best Christian culture, resulting in the finest character and the largest possible use-fulness.

But we cannot dream ourselves into such spiritual attainments; we can only forge them out for ourselves in most heroic, patient, and persistent striving, with the earnest use of the means of grace. Nothing good can be gotten without cost. We must be willing to burn the oil of life if we would give out light.

One step in personal spiritual culture is the giving up and putting off of every wrong thing. It may seem needless to exhort Christians to put away their sins, but even in good lives there may be evil yet cherished which hinders spiritual growth and lessens usefulness. These sins may be so dear to us that we do not care to give them up. Or perhaps we fight against them, but do not overcome them. There are days when we seem to be victorious; we easily master our weakness, and put our besetting vice under our feet. We begin to feel encouraged, thinking that at last the battle is won. Then suddenly, again, we face the old temptations, and lie again in the dust defeated.

If we would have our spiritual life deepened, we must get these sins out of our heart and habit. So long as they stay in us, they will vex and plague us, hindering God's work in us, and marring our usefulness. Unless we expel them, and possess the whole territory of our lives for Christ, we shall not have deep peace, neither shall we become of great use to God. Permitted sins always make men weak. A defeated man cannot help others greatly in their struggles. The reason Jesus Christ is able to succor us in every temptation is because he overcame — he was "in all points tempted, like as we are, yet without sin."

But says some weary struggler, "I cannot master these evils of my heart. When I begin to think I have them subdued, suddenly they rise up again like giants. I cannot expel them."

True, no man can make the conquest of

his own life. But Jesus can do this for us and in us. We do not know what a perfect salvation he is able to give us. We say he saves us from our sins, and we think only of sin's guilt, — that he took upon himself on Calvary the curse that was ours, redeeming us. He did this, and there is therefore now no condemnation to them that are in Christ Jesus. But Christ would save us from our sins in a far deeper way than this. He would save us from the sins themselves, — take them out of our hearts. We may get the victory over all our sins through him who overcame the world. When we have got this mastery, we are ready to be a blessing to others.

Another important element in the process of spiritual culture is to be right both with God and man. For a whole year after David's great sin he was in the black shadows of his transgression. God's hand was heavy upon him. His life was like a drought-smitten field. God's face was hidden.

Neither was he right with men. He had done grievous wrong to many others; he had sinned against the whole nation. But there came a day when his sin was set before him by Nathan's faithful word. Repentance followed; he got right with God and also with man. Then blessing came. God's wonderful forgiveness brought peace and cleansing. David had joy and gladness once more, and the bones which had been broken began to be healed. The Holy Spirit who had been grieved returned to the penitent heart. The joy of salvation was restored. Now David was ready to teach other transgressors God's ways.

Not always are Christians entirely at one with God and man. So long as there are sins unconfessed and unforgiven, there is a cloud shutting out the full sunlight; and so long as there are grudges in the breast, and strivings and contentions with others, the blessing flows not unhindered into our own hearts, nor through us to the lives of others.

It is well that every Christian shall now and then put himself to the test with such questions as these: "Is there anything between my soul and God, anything that separates me from God and hinders closest communion; any evil thing not given up, any sin unconfessed and unforgiven? Is there anything between me and any other soul, anything that hinders complete friendship?" If this testing reveals aught that comes between us and full blessing, we must resolutely put it away, whatever the cost may be, if we would promote our own spiritual culture. We must be right both with God and man, if we would have a rich work of grace in our own hearts, and if we would have God work freely in us in blessing others.

Another essential element in the culture of the spiritual life is prayer. Of course, we all pray. Every Christian prays, — prays every day, prays twice every day. That is, every Christian kneels every morning and evening, and says a prayer. Is it always praying? Is the heart always in the words? Is it a real meeting of the soul with God. Do we not too often merely go over some form of words, into which we put neither thought, desire, faith, nor love? Such praying will never enrich our spiritual lives.

If we look over the names of those who have grown into strength of spiritual character, and have become blessings to men, we shall see that they were all men of prayer. Abraham was a man whose influence has lived all the ages since his time, and he was on such intimate terms with heaven that he was called the friend of God. Moses wrought mightily for the uplifting of the race, and he talked with God as a man talks with a friend. We know what a power Daniel was in the world, what a magnificent character he had, how he stood for God, for truth, and for principle, and did not once fail. Daniel was a man of prayer. Back of his sublime career was his closet, where three times a day he knelt before God.

Or take Jesus. Never was there any other such life of beauty and blessing lived in this world. All these centuries the fragrance of his name has been spreading among the nations, the very saving health of God to millions. Jesus got his strength — that which made his life so victorious, and so rich in its influence — through unbroken communion with God in prayer.

The teaching from all this is that we can never have deep spiritual life without much prayer. A few hurried minutes of formal praying in the morning and a few sleepy moments of saying prayers in the evening, will never bring down into a life any large measure of the love and grace of God. Before we can live deeply we must be on terms of intimacy with Christ. John's life grew and ripened into a rich splendor of spiritual beauty, and we know the secret — he was the close friend of Jesus. We can attain like blessing only by living with Christ, by daily communing with him. No mere formal

devotions will do; there must be a life hid
with Christ in God, a dwelling in the secret
place of the Most High, an abiding in Christ.

One result of such living is the imbuing of
our spirits and characters with the very life of
Christ. If we live ever in his presence his life
will permeate our very being. Another result is spiritual power. We desire to have
influence over men, that we may do them
good. Such power we can get only from God
in prayer. It is not mere personal magnet-
ism, human love, eloquence, earnestness,
enthusiasm for humanity, that will make us
real helpers, comforters, and healers of
others; only the power and grace of God,
received through prayer, can prepare us
for such service.

Bible study is also important in spiritual
culture. It would be interesting to know
how much of God's word most Christians
take into their lives on their average day.
With too many, their ordinary daily devotion
consists in a brief, hurried prayer at the

bedside, with no reading of God's Word. Such devotions will never feed one's soul. If prayer is the "Christian's vital breath," the Bible is the Christian's daily bread. Not to get a portion of it into the heart every day is to starve the soul.

The great men of the Bible were all lovers of God's Word. The people of Israel were taught to read it continually, to hide it in their hearts, and to meditate upon it day and night. Job esteemed the words of God's mouth more than his necessary food. We know where Mary learned the sweet lessons which made her life so beautiful, — she sat at the Master's feet and heard his words, and these words transformed her.

In no way can we ever become rich-hearted Christians, with abundant life, much fruit, and lovely character, but by feeding upon God's Word. Some one writes of the power of a noble thought to make one strong to resist temptation. Another says that one of the secrets of always staying young is to keep new thoughts ever in one's mind. It is wonderful what enriching one gets from familiarity with the best books. But there is no other book whose great thoughts so strengthen one against temptation, so renew one's youth and so enrich one's nature as the Bible. To make it one's daily study is to grow continually in spiritual culture.

There are other ways of deepening spiritual life which might be mentioned. One is faith. It is in believing on Christ that we get the life of Christ into our souls. Obedience is another. Those who do God's will learn more of that will; for, as we follow on, the way is opened to us. Service is another; for love is the law of life, and love can live only in giving and serving. Sorrow and trial are experiences in which the divine intention always is the deepening and enriching of the life. We are not ready to be used in any large way as helpers of others until we have suffered. Most of us have to be broken before we can become bread to hungry souls.

Most of us must learn sympathy and get the gentle touch through suffering of our own.

It is very important that those who lead the young in spiritual things should themselves have a rich experience of the love of Christ. Every teacher should be a close friend of Christ, living with him, coming always from his presence to sit down before the class that waits, eager to be taught and led. We should never be content with small attainments in spiritual things, with a feeble flow of divine life in our souls, with bearing only a little fruit. It is God's will for us that we should attain the highest possible things in spiritual culture, and should bear much fruit.

CHAPTER VIII

THE TEACHER'S BIBLE

A MAN or a woman with a book, is the picture of the Sunday school teacher. The Book is always essential. It is the emblem of the teacher's mission — to declare God's will, to tell of God's love. The message is in the book, and a teacher without his book would seem to be unattested.

Every teacher should have his own Bible. Of course Bibles are all alike, and one finds the same words, whatever the edition, small type or large, limp cover or stiff boards. Still every teacher should have a Bible of his own which he may use daily in his personal reading. It does not seem enough just to pick up any Bible that may be within reach, to-day one, to-morrow another.

A book is like a friend; we learn to love it, and it seems to get to know us better as we use it the longer, and opens its heart to us more and more freely as we commune with it more and more familiarly. It is easier to find what we want in a Bible we have used long — we know just where to look for it, on which page, and where on the page. It is strange, too, how it learns to open at our favorite chapters.

Then the teacher who uses his Bible much and to whom the book becomes a real friend, wishes to mark it, indicating the passages which have helped him, and noting on the margin memoranda and references which may be of value to him in his own spiritual life or in his work with others. Some old and well used Bibles tell the whole spiritual history of those who have read them, in the texts that are underscored. We cannot mark any Bible but our own. Besides, there is something sacred and confidential about the marks one makes in one's own Bible; they tell the story of spiritual experiences which only one's own eye should see. One does not care to put such records of heart-life in any Bible but one's own. It would be making too free with sacred things.

The teacher's Bible should be a good one, one with marginal references, and if possible with its treasury of facts and helps at the end. Some one of the several editions of the Bible which are now so extensively used by teachers and other Christian workers will prove invaluable, having within its covers so much besides the text itself that throws light upon the teachings of the holy Book.

But far more important than the particular edition one uses is the study of the contents of the Bible. Every teacher should be a diligent Bible student. It is not enough to master week by week the passage assigned for the Sunday lesson — this is important, but the teacher should study the Bible in other ways.

How then should he study it? Not the way many persons study it. They open it anywhere, and read a few verses, perhaps a chapter, in one place to-day, and then to-morrow open it, again at random, at another place, and read a few verses or a chapter. So they go on, year after year, perhaps never reading any one book through in order, if at all, often going over the same favorite chapter or some easy psalm again and again. Then they wonder why the Bible is not interesting to them, and why they appear to get so little help from it. How could it be either interesting or helpful, read in such an unscientific manner? No other book would stand the test of such a method of reading. No one could ever get interested in any other book, using it as most persons read the Bible. There is a common-sense way of reading it, however, and to those who adopt this it will yield its deepest revealings and its richest treasures.

The Bible is a collection of booklets bound together in one volume. There are sixty-six of these booklets. They were written by different authors, in different countries, at different times, through some sixteen centuries. The scientific way of studying the Bible is to take it up book by book, mastering the contents of each one in turn. Each has its own history, its own meaning and belongs in its own place. We must know the general facts about the Book before we can properly understand it.

Perhaps we would better begin with the Gospels, since the story of Jesus Christ is the heart of the whole book and the key to it all. Take the Gospel according to Matthew. We may begin by getting all the facts we can find concerning the author. It seems remarkable that a publican should have been chosen to write the first Gospel. Yet no doubt Matthew was specially qualified for this task by his previous education and training. We may notice also that not a word is told about anything that Matthew did or said as an apostle — no act of his is described, no word of his recorded. His Gospel is his only memorial. It would seem that he was called and trained just to write a book. That was his mission.

We may then take up the Gospel itself. It was written for the Jews. Its object was to show them that Jesus of Nazareth was indeed their Messiah who was foretold. It is full of references to the prophecies. Here we have the key to this Gospel.

Having learned all such available facts, the next thing is to read the book — not a few words here and there to-day, and a few to-morrow, but to go through the whole of it, if possible at one reading. This should be done several times, until the student is familiar with every fact and incident recorded.

Let the same course be followed with the other books until each one has been mastered. This will require a considerable time, but it will be time well spent. The teacher who takes up the Bible in this systematic way will get an intelligent idea of it as a book. He will know where each booklet belongs in the history and will be able to fit it into its place.

Nor is it so formidable a task as one might imagine — this reading of the several books of the Bible through at single sittings. No one who takes the Book up in this manner, with enthusiasm, earnestness and reverence, will ever regret it. The impression derived from reading, for example, one of the Gospels through at a single sitting, is wonderfully inspiring. It gives us in one picture a view of the whole of the life of Christ on the earth.

But there is another study of the Scriptures which is even more important for the teacher's spiritual benefit than by this method. Thousands who have never known anything of the Bible as literature, have yet found in it the treasures of life. They have never mastered it book by book; but they have had a key wherewith to open its storehouses when they will, finding therein divine revealings, heavenly comforts, promises for life's way, counsels for every duty and perplexity. However well we may learn to know the Bible as a book, we need most of all to know it as the Word of God, and to learn how to find in it bread for our souls' hunger.

One good way of studying the Bible for spiritual profit is by the topical method. We may take a particular subject and find from all parts of the Scriptures all that bears upon it, or will throw any light upon it. For example, take God's forgiveness. There are many superficial notions on this subject. Many make it altogether, too easy a matter, to be forgiven, having no thought of the divine holiness or of the real meaning of sin. Trace the subject of forgiveness through the Scriptures, getting the light of all the great passages on it. The result of such a study will be a deepened sense of the guilt of sin, new visions of the divine holiness, a fresh impression of the meaning of the cross, and then a wonderful view of the fullness and completeness of the forgiveness which God bestows upon all who confess their sins and accept Jesus Christ as their Redeemer.

Or take a series of studies on the character

of God — his holiness, his love, his grace, his fatherly care. Or find out what the Bible has to say about the Christian life, what it is to be a Christian, the Christian's privileges, duties, and responsibilities, or the promises may be sought out and gathered into clusters. Special studies of much interest and profit will be found in looking up such words as peace, joy, hope, faith, love.

This topical method of Bible reading yields valuable results, if it is pursued reverently and thoroughly. It enables us to see the many sides of truth and thus to get a better conception of it, for as a rule no one text shows us the whole of any inspired teaching. Wrong views are often held by superficial Bible readers because they have taken their impressions from a single verse, instead of getting all the light upon the subject which they could find in the whole book, and then gathering from this the final teaching.

For this topical study, a concordance and a Bible textbook are the only helps required.

The concordance shows all the passages in which the word itself occurs. Besides these, there usually are other passages which treat of the topic or bear upon it, and these a good textbook will indicate. It is profitable also to follow out in a reference Bible the various references for each verse turned to, as ofttimes these will throw additional light upon the subject.

All this requires much time and thought, but the results will richly repay the devout student. It is a search for gold and gems, in which one's quest is never in vain. The Bible is the Word of God and no painstaking study should be thought too laborious, if it brings out in clearer light the truth about God and about duty.

Besides this serious and thorough study of the Bible, to learn the mind and will of God, every teacher needs to maintain the habit of daily Bible reading as a devotional exercise. Thus he hears God's voice in instruction, in correction, in warning, in guidance, in comfort, in inspiration — learning the lessons for his own life as he needs to know them. Thus only can the Word become a lamp to his feet and a light to his path. Every morning should have its verse, which may stay all day in the heart, like a grain of rich perfume to sweeten all the day's life.

The teacher's Bible is meant for use. It is not enough that he shall know its inspired words; they must be taken into his life, believed, trusted in as sure words, leaned on as one would lean on the bosom of Christ himself, and obeyed as the very will of God.

The Bible is a book which requires two kinds of interpretation to make its teachings clear. Commentaries are good in their way. They tell us what the words mean and explain all the allusions. But however perfectly one may understand the Bible passages, so far as language is concerned, it requires experience to reveal the full meaning that lies in the words. There are promises of comfort, but we do not know their preciousness until we are in sorrow. There are words for the widow, for the orphan, for the poor, for the sick, for the old, but we cannot find the real blessing in these words until we are in the experience for which the promise was given.

Hence the Bible opens its hidden meanings only as life goes on. We find what we need in some peculiar experience, in an old verse we had read a hundred times before without seeing the meaning which now flashes out so bright and clear.

CHAPTER IX

THE TEACHER AND THE HOLY SPIRIT

WITHOUT the help of the Holy Spirit no one is ready to be a teacher of God's Word. No matter how well trained he may be, how familiar he is with the truths he is to present, until he has received the Holy Spirit, he is not prepared to teach. The disciples had been for many months with their Master. They had lived in closest intimacy with him. They had received the truth from his own lips. They had been under his personal training. Yet they were bidden not to go out to begin their work until they had received power from on high.

In like manner, those who would now become teachers of others, must wait for the heavenly power. Specific training is important. They should study the Bible, so as to know what they are to teach. No one is ready to sit down before a class until he has some reasonable knowledge of the way of salvation. How can one teach others what one has not himself learned? How can one guide inexperienced feet along paths over which one has never yet himself walked? How can a teacher lead his pupils to a Saviour he has not found for himself? How can he make plain to eager, inquiring minds, truths concerning life which he himself has never learned by experience?

In honoring the Holy Spirit, we must take care not to dishonor the Holy Word. To claim to depend upon the Spirit while we make no use of the sacred Scriptures is fanaticism. The Spirit uses the Word of God. It is important that the teacher shall know his Bible well. The minds and hearts of the first disciples were filled with the words of Christ. This was not sufficient in itself to prepare them for their mission as apostles — it was necessary after they had been so instructed, that the Holy Spirit should come into their hearts as the fire of God to kindle all this knowledge into a glowing flame; and yet the knowledge was essential. The apostles were to be witnesses of Christ and they could be witnesses only of what they knew. The Spirit did not teach them new truths — he only vitalized the truth they knew before.

The teacher must know the truths he is to teach. He may not expect the Holy Spirit to reveal them to him. There is no promise of this. No teacher has any right to omit Bible study and the preparation of his lesson, and then expect the Spirit to supply the lack, to teach him what he has not taken the pains to learn for himself. Sometimes one hears a teacher or a preacher quote a word of Jesus which says, "Be not anxious how or what ye shall speak: for it shall be given you in that hour what ye shall speak," as if it were a discouragement or a forbidding of preparation beforehand for speaking God's message. But this is a perversion of Scripture. We must get the meaning of the words of Christ in their connection, and not tear out fragments and interpret them as if they were independent sayings. It was of their defense before rulers, and not of their preaching, that Jesus was then speaking to his disciples. We must learn of Christ and know his teachings, and then we have a right to expect the Holy Spirit to come and fill us, and kindle our knowledge of Christ into a glowing fire.

Nor again, must we expect that the Spirit will make the training of the teacher unnecessary. An educated ministry is not unscriptural. Sometimes we hear it said, as an argument against careful training of ministers, and teachers, that the apostles were ignorant, unlearned men, that Jesus passed by the educated classes and took for his first disciples a company of rude fishermen who had never been in the schools of the rabbis. But those who use this as a reason against the educating of ministers and teachers for their work, overlook the fact that for two or three years these men were under Christ's own personal training. He was their teacher, and never was there another such instructor as he. No class of students in any theological seminary ever had such training as had the apostles of Christ.

It will not do therefore to claim that teachers need no training in order to be ready for their work in the Sunday school; that all they require is to be filled with the Holy Spirit, and that then they will be ready to do skillful teaching. There is not a word in the New Testament to support such a claim. It is not promised that the Spirit will take a man who has no education, no mental discipline, and at once transform him into an eloquent preacher. Now and then something like this may seem to be done — an un-lettered, untrained man may be brought to Christ and almost immediately may become a successful winner of souls. But this is not the usual divine method. Men need to be educated and trained to prepare them for their work as teachers of the gospel. We need for this work not only good men and women, filled with the Spirit, but men and women who have been prepared for their holy ministry in the wisest and most skillful way.

Nor again, does the Holy Spirit work independently of Christ. Christ came first, revealing the Father, declaring the divine will, and giving his life for man's redemption. When his work was finished, and he had returned to heaven, the Spirit came. But his mission was to glorify Christ, to take of the things of Christ and show them to men. He did not speak of himself, but poured the light of divine revealing upon the person and work of the Redeemer.

This truth must not be overlooked by those who are engaged in Christian teaching. The Spirit honors Christ and presents his person and work. We are to seek to bring souls to Christ, not to the Holy Spirit.

What then is the Christian teacher's

relation to the Spirit? First of all, it is
personal. He needs the work of the Spirit
in his own heart and life. He must be a
Christian before he is a teacher, and when
he accepts Jesus Christ as his Saviour and
Lord, he receives the Spirit. All the work
of grace in his heart is wrought by the divine
Spirit. Just in the measure in which he
surrenders himself to the Spirit, will his
Christian life grow in intensity and power.
It is the work of the Spirit to pour light upon
the inner life, that we may discover the evil
of our nature and then put it away. It
is the part of faith to yield the whole being
to the sway of the Spirit, that he may
cleanse the heart and transform the life
into the beauty of Christ.

There are many words in the New Testament which indicate the closeness of the
relation into which the third person of the
Trinity enters with every believer. For
example, Paul exhorts Christians not to
grieve the Holy Spirit. This implies that

the Spirit is a person, for we cannot grieve
an influence. He comes to us as our friend.
He is a divine guest who would make our
hearts his home. We grieve him when we
fail in hospitality to him. To shut him out of
any part of our lives is to grieve him. Any
word, act or thought of ours which is not
cordial, loyal and loving, grieves him. When
we resist his work in us, his work of convic-
tion, of the discovery and casting out of sin,
his work of cleansing and purifying, or his
work of quickening and inspiring, we grieve
him. The Holy Spirit should be allowed to
work unhindered and unopposed in every
part of our lives, and we give him joy and
comfort when we make our surrender to him
so complete that he finds nothing in the way
of his taking full possession of our being.

It is this personal relation of the believer
to the Holy Spirit which is first in importance.
The teacher should be holy in heart and life.
He should be wholly under the influence of
the Spirit. He should be filled unto all the

fullness of God. It is this that will give him power, and not any special influence of the Spirit which he may receive as a Christian worker. The teacher should be filled with the Holy Spirit; this will make him a new man and prepare him to be a successful winner of souls.

Then, besides this personal relation as believers in Christ, those who would teach others should seek the special help of the Spirit in their work. The apostles were not permitted to go into the field to tell the story of the redemption until they had been endued with power from on high. When they had received this enduement they at once began to speak with new tongues. This gift was supernatural, but we may learn from it that those who would speak now for Christ to others need a new power of speech. The receiving of the Holy Spirit will not enable them to speak in a language they have never learned, but it will give to their words a spiritual energy which they have never had before. A burning heart produces burning speech. Those who obtain the help of the Holy Spirit in teaching the Word of God will find that their words have new force. God himself will speak through them, and his voice of gentle stillness will reach the hearts of those they teach as no eloquent words of mere human speech can ever do.

How may the teacher obtain this help of the Holy Spirit in his work? As has been said already, the teacher must be Christian. He must abide in Christ and have Christ abiding in him. Then, he must seek the guidance of the Spirit in his preparation for teaching. Only the Spirit can reveal the meaning of the words of the Scriptures, for He is their author — they were inspired by him. It is the reverent, prayerful student of the Scriptures who finds the precious things in them.

Again, the teacher should seek the aid of the Spirit in preparing the hearts of his pupils to receive the truths he is to teach them. He should also make sure of the Spirit in himself before he begins his work, going from his closet to his class. Then, when he is in his place, with the Bible open, he should depend upon the Spirit to use him and his words, to speak through him and to work in the hearts of his pupils.

Those who teach thus, filled with the Holy Spirit and under his power, will never work in vain. They will be burning and shining lights, shining because they burn.

THE "SILENT TIMES" SERIES

Solid Ground Christian Books is delighted to announce its intention to begin publishing The "Silent Times" Series by J.R. Miller. We plan to publish the following titles:

Silent Times
Strength and Beauty
Week-day Religion
The Garden of the Heart
Making the Most of Life
The Building of Character
The Joy of Service
Things to Live For
Personal Friendships of Jesus
Life's Open Door: A Book of Comfort

We are convinced that the works of J.R. Miller will prove to be a source of encouragement to weary souls who are battling every day with the world, the flesh and the devil. Pray that the Lord will enable us to bring back these books that can instruct this generation in the ways of God.

OTHER SOLID GROUND TITLES

A Pastor's Sketches 1 & 2 by Ichabod Spencer who was known as 'The Bunyan of Brooklyn' during his remarkable ministry in that great city. These volumes are changing lives all over the world as they instruct those who minister to troubled souls in every walk of life. Three seminaries are now using it. $12.95 each

God's Outlaw: The Story of William Tyndale and the English Bible by Brian Edwards has sold out several times since its first printing in 1976. This book is must reading for all who desire to know the price that was paid that we might have the Bible in our own language. This is a soul stirring book. $13.95

Golden Hours: Heart-Hymns of the Christian Life by Elizabeth Prentiss. This is the spiritual autobiography in verse of this godly woman from a former day. She is best known for her book *Stepping Heavenward* and her hymn *More Love to Thee, O Christ*. This is a book for sufferers and those who care for them. $9.95

King of the Cannibals: The Story of John G. Paton by Jim Cromarty. This is an amazing account of the life and labors of one of the greatest missionaries of the 19th century. Stuart Olyott says, *"No one can read this book and remain the same."* John MacArthur says, *"Cromarty's lively writing style makes this a book that is hard to put down."* It is an especially fine book to use for Family Worship. $14.95

Legacy of a Legend: Spiritual Treasure from the Heart of Edward Payson. This is a volume to be read and reread as long as you are on this earth, as this great man of God from the past opens his heart on dozens of themes from Scripture and life. Payson was the father of Elizabeth Prentiss and her greatest hero. $9.95

Mothers of the Wise and Good by Jabez Burns was written in 1846 to honor the role of the mother in the home. Brief biographical sketches are given of such wise and good men as Augustine, Jonathan Edwards, John Newton, Philip Doddridge and dozens of others, with special emphasis upon the influence their mothers had upon their lives. This is a book to challenge and encourage mothers. $8.95

Opening Up Ephesians by Peter Jeffery is the first in a series of straightforward expositions of New Testament books intended especially for those in the formative years of their Christian life. Although written with young people in mind this is a series that will benefit anyone who wants to grow in grace. $9.95

Stepping Heavenward by Elizabeth Prentiss is a wonderful book that has sold over 100,000 copies since reappearing in 1992. It is one of Elisabeth Elliot's all time favorite books, and is highly recommended by Kay Arthur, Susan Hunt, Martha Peace and Joni Eareckson Tada. A truly life-changing book. $10.95

The Person and Work of the Holy Spirit by Benjamin B. Warfield is a book that contains all the sermons, articles and book reviews on the Holy Spirit by one of the greatest theologians of the late 1800's and early 1900's. Warm reading. $10.95

call us toll free at **1-877-666-9469**
e-mail us at solid-ground-books@juno.com